So Much Inside

by

Stephanie R. Barry

First printing

Lulu.com has allowed this work to remain exactly as the author intended, verbatim, without editorial input.

ISBN: 978-1-105-11740-4

PUBLISHED BY LULU.COM
www.lulu.com

Printed in the United States of America

Dedication

So Much Inside is dedicated to all those women or men who felt like everything was taken away by being a victim of rape, ridicule, missing love of a parent or parents, emotional, verbal and physical abuse. I am a personal witness that it can scar your life but it has no grounds to taking your soul. As women we nurture by nature and that is a God given gift that should not be trampled over and taken for granted. God does love us even though he allows trials and tribulations in our lives. He never promised us heaven on earth, only peace in heaven. I know that many of us feel God should keep certain things from happening but the thing to realize is that God never puts more on us than we can bear. If something you go through actually kills you than how are you here to still tell it and talk about it. In that case it was an experience; one that made you stronger and gives you the courage to reach out to others who will understand what it may feel like to hold "So Much Inside" and motivate them to "take back their soul."

Chapter 1

So Much Inside

Living in West Alabama was not easy for Shelly, with being ridiculed, lied on, considered an outcast and teased all the time; it is a wonder she's still in her right mind. Shelly has been abused in every way one can think of but she still moved forward in her life. From a little girl up she had to deal with the most important men in her life emotionally, mentally and some even physically abusing her. She had to deal with friends and family setting her up for failure without just cause. It was hard but she survived. It was dangerous but she keeps heart all while holding "So Much Inside." Shelly had to realize what she was doing to herself and stop it. Although Shelly thought she was moving forward the stains of her past kept her bound and she was painting an ugly picture in every relationship allowed. Shelly had to often go back and write down her life to try and get to the bottom of her pain and this was the beginning of her losing her own self made demons.

Shelly writes, "I have to go back to the very beginning to "build a heavenly fortune and stop creating an earthly monster." As Shelly briefly reminisces over her entire life she writes: every since I was a little girl, one thing has never left me, and that is knowing who God is, his protection and his love. All of my life I have been hated, mocked, picked on, lied on, cheated, deceived and a bunch of other stuff but through it all I remained humbled and in God. So many people have looked into my life and many make judgment but others crave to be in my shoes. I laugh because no one can handle my shoes. To begin, I knew I was always a special person; I have stood out like no other. It began the day I came from the hospital eating popsicle; which my family tells me the story all the time. My mom said I had to have it and my sister Angie reminds me often. I smile because by the breath of the Holy Spirit I came out strong. My walk with God started early in life and the devil has been trying to kill me a long time. He has sent his advocates to talk about me, hate me, deceive me, cheat me and many other things. The things I have been through, many would have lost their mind and given up long time ago. I was raped at 13, hurt by family, friends & men whom I have loved. I have had people envy me without valid reason except satan was using them to try and break me down. People lying on me, loosing family, money, jobs, house, cars and being brought down to nothing. What the devil has meant for bad, God has meant it for good. Had God not allowed those things, I would not pray like I do. I would be too consumed with the riches and people in my life. God allowed me to get married and disprove everyone who wanted me to never have companionship but it was also a lesson in it for me. I ran off to a different state after marrying while bringing along the devil of a man right with me. After he broke me down and I went through extreme heartache and pain, I divorced and ran to another new city and state to start a new life. Little did I know, satan sent his advocates after me; I had a man who tried to make me prostitute to live; he tried to strip me of everything, even my mind and I got pregnant and miscarried for a man who wanted me to abort. God needed my attention and I was letting other things and people consume it. I needed to get rid of some things and people. Once God broke me down and stripped me of almost everything He allowed me to get, my eyes opened wide and I began to change. My life began to pick up after I obeyed God and made some moves closer in Him! I don't have a lot of money, I don't have a fancy car, I don't live in a fancy apartment or house but what I have is the love of God and his protection. I have used a few curse words, raised my voice as high as it can go and also been in a few fights but never did I forget who God is. I grew up in the church; Holiness to began, ending in Church of God and Christ, just titles. The real reason I still love and live is because of God! If it had to be based off of church folk and regular people, I would have fallen long time ago. I would not be here today, "But God!"

Shelly offered a prayer and warning in her writing to those who needed to know God is calling out to His chosen ones. She writes; My prayer is: If anyone is living with all your material things and allowing those things to consume your time from God, don't wait for God to strip you of it to get your attention and for you to be real! It is time to recognize that we are living in Revelations, God is raising his people and you can be in or out! It is only two choices, Heaven or Hell?

After Shelly finishes writing down the major points of her past hurt and pain and showing how God has been there with her through it all she reminisces deeper into detail of every account of her life as trouble began to mount. Shelly remembers back to fourth grade and all the children had to make some bonnet hats. Her mom bought her some silk pink material and the teacher helps her as she did with the other fourth grade girls to make their hats. The girls in the class became jealous because Shelly's hat was made with pink silk and they pushed Shelly's next door neighbor and friend, who shared the class with her, up to fight Shelly; ending their friendship."What a shame?" She thought about when she was thirteen and the hell she went through! As many didn't know but her virginity was taken by a boy she entrusted her life as she told no one! She thought about how she almost got ate up by a German Sheppard one day walking from her grandmother's house because a boy in her neighborhood who likes her was pissed because she wouldn't pay him any attention. To Shelly he was too much older and she was not ready to date. Shelly ended up having to fight this one girl because the boy the young girl wanted Shelly and instead of getting mad with him, the young girl turned her anger to Shelly. Shelly got lied on a lot by guys and girls in reference to her sexual behavior. Kids were very cruel as one guy who many teased Shelly about in the seventh and eighth grade had put out a rumor that she performed sexual favors for him. Many thought Shelly was out there as they call it. Truly they knew nothing about her and according to many; Shelly should have had fifty babies at an early age. Shelly thinks about how a lot of that stuff scarred her mentally and she could not wait to finish high school so she could move away and prove them wrong. Instead she got caught up in this imaginary living to disprove others only to disprove herself, "but GOD!"

Chapter 2

He Took My Soul

Shelly goes into visual detail of her rape and the events afterwards that carried her down a life of doom soulfully, spiritually, mentally, physically and emotionally. Shelly accounts each moment and the dramatic feelings behind it all.

On a sunny day in 1989, I was just a little thirteen year old with long thick pigtails. I was only thirteen but I can remember that I had the body of an eighteen year old, smooth pecan colored skin tone and light brown eyes. Just a small innocent thirteen year old who thought about keeping my honor roll status in junior high school and taking care of my mom. The baby of six kids; two brothers and three sisters and family had just moved out of the projects into our new home which was about five minutes of walking distance from the junior high school. My family had just moved into a five bedrooms, two bathrooms home. My mother and father were proud to be home owners. See the story is that neither mother nor father had beyond a sixth grade education. They were victims of the cotton picking time but to my parents, they had accomplished what people say they couldn't. I always valued the strength my mother showed even though she didn't know how to read or spell. She made things happen by trusting in God. That was all I needed to see. Remembering the day mom was told by the Holy Spirit that her house had been approved, and mom was sitting outside with her two friends on the porch as the kids play in the yard. I remember mommy jumping up out of nowhere in the middle of conversation with her friends and saying, "Thank you God, clapping her hands and repeating,

"My house has been approved!" Moms' friends looked at her strange and began to laugh and call her crazy for the outburst but low and behold, God had spoken and minutes later a phone call came and the approval was passed. Those friends ended in having to apologize. My grandmother was a God-fearing woman who had been in church a long time and this is where my mother standing ground came from. There was only one thing wrong in this picture though, mom and grandmother didn't have a solid mother and daughter relationship. To dig deeper into the story, mother grew up in a time where brothers, aunts, uncles, cousins, sisters and several people lived in a home together. Mom and I had a very close relationship, so she talked with me in a way that she didn't feel she could talk with the other kids. After all, I seemed special; something was different about my level of care and love. I taught my mother to read at the age of four. I could always feel when mother was sad even though she would try to hide it. Mom was sitting in the bedroom one day alone and seeming to be very quiet which was unusual. I was use to watching my mother in the kitchen preparing dinner for my father or having girl talk with her friends, as they all lived in the same housing area. They would often be sitting on one another's porches just chatting away. They did plenty of man bashing, if I must say but this particular day, mom was alone in her room. As I eased from behind the wall into my mother's room, I could hear her silently crying and the tears were rolling down my mother's cheek. "Mommy," I call out, what's wrong? I was curious to know what was making mom whom I knew as a very happy and strong woman, cry. My mother began to wipe tears from her cheeks and tell me that everything was okay. I replied, "Mom, I don't believe that because you are crying and I have never seen you cry." "What's wrong mommy?" My mom grabs me as she takes a deep breath and swallowed. She is now holding me in her arms. I am still not understanding or having knowledge to what brought my mother to tears. With a confused look on my face, I ask; one more time, "Mom please tell me what is wrong!" My mother asks me to sit down beside her and grabs my hand as I take a seat on the side of her bed. "Shelly, "my mom says, what I am about to share with you is something I have dared to share with anyone. I know that you are young and may not understand a lot of what mommy is about to discuss but because of your heart and your concern unlike most thirteen year olds, I will share this with you. Mom tells me that every day when looking into my eyes she is reminded of herself as a young girl. She tells me that she feels like I am a younger her getting a second chance in life. She goes on to tell me how long time ago when she was eleven that she was raped by a cousin and that she never told anybody because she felt no one would believe her. She never felt her voice was big enough or loud enough to anyone to hear her cry or believe it. She stated that her mother was loving but not loving or protective enough in her eyes. Mom details the story; "One night as she slept in the bed between cousins, sisters, and brothers, she awake to a hand over her mouth and her cousin lifting her gown up and spreading open her legs. He was so much older than she was and said he would kill her if she made a move or sound. Mom said she laid there silently in much pain as he raped and molested her. At the time she states she didn't know exactly what was happening, she just knew it was not right. The older male cousin told her to never tell anyone or he would kill her and make her story a lie. He told her that they would look at her as being a bad person therefore she kept silent all these years. Mother says to me; baby girl, what I have shared today is something that has bothered me for years and I just want to find the strength and courage to protect each of you from that type of harm. I love you Shelly and always know that you can come to me. I believe in all of my kids. I will always believe your story and investigate. As mother and I conclude our conversation my father walks into the room. "What's going on here," my father says? Mother responded by saying she was giving me a one on one about events that can be life changing. I proceed to leaving the room as my father greets mom with a kiss. For many reasons, I was not as close to my father as I was with my mother. Being that I was a very smart and curious child, I along with my sisters and brothers observed our father drinking, being verbally abusive and smoking behavior, not only that, he was a cheater. I overheard my mom plenty in talking with her friends about how her father was caught with another woman. In growing up my sisters and I witnessed our father not wanting us to have friends or be around any of the neighborhood kids. I got the bulk of my father's name calling and verbal abuse. He would tell me such things as, "you think you so pretty, you think you smart and telling me that I was fast and needed a beating. To be my father, he didn't seem to like me at all. These are the things that made me shy away from my father as I didn't understand why he treated me this way.

After I leave the room, I go outside with all of my other siblings to play. I played football that evening with the other kids and had a wonderful day. I was confident and loving life. My mom was friends with a young woman who had a host of kids and became friends with the eldest son who was fifteen, finding in the end we were kinfolk. Me, my sisters and brothers would always go and play with these kids when mom would go by their house. Everyone became close like brothers and sisters. Being associated with this elder son started a lifetime of trouble for me. I was very comfortable with Cedrick, the eldest son and we played together all the time, talked all the time and shared a lot. Cedrick was a handsome young fifteen year old, fair skinned with hazel eyes. He was my protector as we would walk to school together and often I and my siblings stayed the night at his mom or my mom's house. One day as I had walked over to my grandma's house to get a Popsicle, I came across Cedrick. He was by the junior high school and asks me to walk up by the school with him so that we may walk through the short cut back to my home. Of course I had no objections because I trusted him and we were family. We walked up through the buildings of the junior high school talking about moments we had that were so funny. Thinking of one particular time where Cedrick burnt his thumb while running out of the house with a hot fiery pan from the stove to remove it from the home to keep it from causing extensive fire damage. He laughed and I chuckled as he stated he knew nothing more to do but run out of the house with the fiery pan. I in the middle of our moment of laughter remembered I needed to get home. It was turning dusk and my mom would miss me if I didn't return home soon. As I began to walk away, Cedrick grabbed my hand. With a strange look I asked, "What is going on?" He looked at me with a smile and told me he liked me. I eased my hand out of his and said, "I like you to Cedrick!" You are like a brother to me. I then turn my back and say to him, come on, let's go. Cedrick grabbed me by the arm once more and said, "I really do like you and I want you to be my girl. At this moment, I was confused, saying; "We are cousins!" My mom and your mom are not just friends, we are blood related. Cedrick then stated to me that he did not care while confessing he has very strong feelings of love for me. I began to walk away and Cedrick grabs me, pin me up against the schools brick wall. I am scared and starting to fear the worst. "What are you doing Cerdrick," I ask as I scramble to get loose. He kisses me and I resist but cannot get away. As Cedrick held my hands together on the wall he lets go only to grab for my pant button. I am in disbelief and cannot believe this is happening. All the time he is smiling with those big hazel brown eyes opened wide as to be excited. I could see the spirit of the devil in his eyes for he is a different boy then I entrusted my life to. He was my brother, my cousin and my friend, just not at this moment. Cedrick pins one of my hands back up against the wall and rips my pant button loose with his other hand. He began to pull down my pants as I struggle with him to keep him from pulling them down. I began to cry as my heart was racing and I was out of breath. I is so hurt that I can feel myself weakening with fear of what was about to happen. I call out for help but no one can hear me as I realize, it's the weekend, Sunday and no one is near to hear me cry, scream or holler. I try to reason with Cedrick to not do me like this but he kept pulling at my pants with an evil smile. For one moment I thought I had reached him because he stopped and said, "I was just kidding around! You were scared weren't you?" I was crying, breathing hard and weak in the knees. I dared to say anything further and began to walk away quickly. As I turned my back, he quickly snatched me around, pulled my pants and panties down as I fell backwards to the ground, helpless and full of fear. Cedrick, as I struggled to get a grip on my pants and panties to pull them up would not let it happen. He held my hands with one of his hands, planted his lips against mine and eagerly inserted his penis inside of me. It was a struggle as I squirmed in trying to get away. I tried to slide upward away from him to keep him from inserting me but I felt my skin being torn from the concrete. I was in pain both ways. Cedrick was taking my virginity and as I screamed and cried, thoughts were flashing back to my mother's tears and conversation. This was not happening, in a daze, as I tried to imagine while Cedrick kept pushing and forcing himself inside of me. To keep me quiet, he forced kisses onto my mouth. He continued pushing and pushing for what seem like forever and finally it was over. After the horrifying moment I lay there in shock and disbelief. Many things ran through my mind as I felt extremely defiled. In my thoughts I am thinking, "I cannot believe this has happened, is this a bad dream? My father is going to say it was my fault because he feels I am a fast tale girl. My mom will be torn to pieces if she realizes she could not protect me. I no longer have something special to give to anyone, I am ruined, I was thinking. I didn't know what to do but what I did know was that I didn't want to destroy my mother's heart. Cedrick left me there alone as I gathered myself together and wiped away tears. I saw the blood on the ground from being torn and raped, cleaned myself up as much as I could and gained my composure. I walked home as I felt pain in my vagina, eased into the house acting as if everything was normal, went into my room and turned music on as I normally do. My mom was familiar with this and loved to her Shelly sing along with the music. I spent hours many times in listening to music and singing songs. My mom knocked at my door because she wanted to see my face and acknowledge me. I opened the door and mom asked if everything was okay. It was as if she could feel something was wrong. I gave a big fake smile and said, "No, everything is okay!" Mom wanted to ask more questions but I stated that I was just listening to music and my favorite song was playing, so mom looking puzzled just walked off, telling me to clean up because dinner would be ready soon. That was my queue to take a shower and remove the filth from my body. As I proceeded to the bathroom I took my soiled panties with me and washed them by hand. I had decided I would clean up all evidence and not say anything to anybody. While in the bathroom taking a shower I allowed the tears to roll along with the water. I felt dirty, disgusted, heartbroken and confused. I was building up hate towards Cedrick as I thought about what he has done to me. I want to tell someone but I fear hurting so many people and allowing my father to be able to point the finger at me. I decide to let go and let God! After, I finish showering; I went into the kitchen to eat dinner with my parents and siblings as they all gathered. I was not comfortable in sitting because my vagina was in pain but I played it off as much as I could. My mother at one point looked over and asked; Shelly, why are you frowning and seeming to be in deep thought instead of eating? For a moment I wanted to just blurt it out, holler and cry instead I softly stated, "I am just being thankful for the food and presence of family." Mom gave a questionable look but let it go.

After dinner that night I went back into my room to play more music and cry about what had been done. I had to see this boy at school the next day as wondered how I was going to feel and what I would do to make sure I wasn't alone anywhere with him. I cried myself to sleep that night and arose the next morning to get ready for school. I did my regular hour of getting ready in anticipation of having to see this boy "Cedrick" who has defiled me. I arrive at the junior high school and guess who would be the first person I see, Cedrick! Inside my mind, I am screaming "o my God!" I want to run but all things would be questionable. Standing there in fear without words, he reaches out to me as if things are normal and I yell, "Don't touch me!" Others look around and I began feeling ashamed, dropping my head, not being able to look at him any longer, silently tells him to never touch me again as I walks off. He gives me this evil grin and walks in the opposite direction. My friend Trish walks up to me and asks, "What was going on?" Trish states to me that she has never seen that face on me before, she ask again, "Shelly are you okay?" I grab Trish, give her a big hug as my heart is beating extremely fast and states Cedrick is not a good person. I was careful not to go into detail but made sure Trish knew I never wanted to be near Cedrick ever again. I went for a while after that incident without crossing the path of Cedrick until one day when I was hanging out with Shavonne and Sally; two other friends of mine. These two girls were cousins and I felt they were pretty good friends until that day. I had on this blue jean button up long skirt the day of hanging with Shavonne and Sally. They told me they wanted to go over to my house but they wanted to cut through the back of the school as it was a short cut to get there faster. They claimed they didn't want to walk the long way around, I questioned but agreed. As Shavonne, Sally and I started to go up the road towards the school, Shavonne and Sally started to pull at my skirt in a playful manner, almost pulling it off. I ask repeatedly for them to stop as my skirt almost completely came off. By this time we were on the school campus by the trailers in the back end. Guess who jumps out of one of the empty unused classroom trailers, Cedrick and two other boys, all whom I knew. "Damn," I am thinking, this is a set up! Once again I am facing this wide, hazel eye boy, knowing what is about to happen as

Shavonne and Sally run off while these three boys surround me. I know I was in trouble; calling out to Shavonne and Sally, begging for help as I am carried into one of the empty trailers by the three boys. I yell to Cedrick, "Why are you doing this to me as he and the other boys just laugh and grin as if everything was a joke. While one boy held my hands the other held my legs and the third took off her skirt and panties. It was Cedrick, making sure he was the first as they rotated in what they call, "the train!" Those boys were raping me and all I could do was cry. I begged and begged until Cedrick finally spoke and said stop as one of the boys were about to stick a tree limb inside of me. I was ruined for life and once again I could not tell a soul for the embarrassment and pain. These boys told me they would kill me if she told anyone as this was adding insult to injury. Once again with bloody soiled panties, I went home. As I arrived home, I could see the family car not there, walking in the house to realize mom and dad were out grocery shopping and feeling relieved that I could wipe away the struggle before anyone would notice. My brothers and sisters asked me what was wrong with me and I lied and stated I had been in a fight with Shavonne and Sally, although it wasn't true, I wished it had been. I cleansed myself up and at that moment I realized I could trust no one, male or female. My so called friends had set me up for failure and refused to help me. As young as I was I had enemies and didn't know why. I cried like a baby, yet silent in my pain would not go anywhere without my brothers, sisters or parents. I would not hang out with or talk with Shavonne or Sally anymore even when they would come or call to the house. My mom inquired to why I didn't want to hang out with the girls anymore and I replied with saying, they were not good friends. Soon Sally and Shavonne stopped calling and coming by as they had finally got the picture about the trouble I had to face that day because of them. Being that I never went anywhere alone ever again or trusted any of my so-called friends, I was safe. Even when my mom would visit Cedrick's mom I would stay at home. I consumed myself into music and writing poetry, music lyrics and short stories; for this became my hobby.

About two months later, I heard Cedrick had made his way sexually through many other females around my age group, many who were classmates of mines. One night as I slept I heard a knock at my window, my screen was being removed and it was Cedrick coming through the window. He was one bold rapist and seems to care about nothing except taking what he wanted. He told me to be quiet or he would hurt me. It was summer time and unfortunately my window was up so he had easy access to getting in. He wanted me to have sex; he wanted to destroy me all over again in my own bedroom. I wasn't about to let this happen and while I built rage as Cedrick stands in my room, I whispers, "I need to go to the bathroom first and make sure my mom and dad are sleep. Cedrick agreed as I contemplated; thinking, "I got him now," in my mind planning to tell and alert my parents. I was not afraid of finally taken action without exposing the full truth of my rape. I went outside of the room, closed the door slightly behind myself, snuck right into my mother and father room and advised someone was in there. Cedrick must have heard them coming because right before they pushed the door open, he jumped out of the window with curtain blinds and all going with him. My father had his gun ready to shoot but Cedrick had disappeared. I had even given his name in speculation. I said, "it was Cedrick ma, I know it was! I heard he had been going around to several other girls in my class windows. That night I went to sleep in her sisters' room and feeling relieved that he didn't get the chance to defile me again, I slept with no worries. Being that it was summertime I didn't have to worry about having to see or confront him until my mom went to talk with his mom and he was punished. I went on for a year not being alone or hanging with any female friends.

Chapter 3

Dating Years

A year later at age 14, I called myself being in a real true relationship as my mom did not oppose me dating a seventeen year old named Jeremy. Jeremy and I got together in a very odd way. I, my sister Angie and Tessa would always go to the junior high school basketball games as they were playing rival teams from different cities and counties. This particular seventeen year old was on the Livingston junior high basketball team and somehow I caught his eye. At this time I was eleven and he was fourteen. He told me that since that day he had always sought to find me and become my boyfriend. How we meet up again was through a phone conversation my sister Tessa was having with his cousin; her boyfriend, not knowing who Jeremy was. As Jeremy sat in the background asking his cousin to ask Tessa if she had a sister he could date, Tessa offered up me. My sister who was eighteen at the time allowed me to have conversation with her boyfriend's cousin and low and behold it was Jeremy. Jeremy decided to come see me along with Tessa's boyfriend whom was his cousin. Jeremy was seventeen with his own ride and own money, tall dark-skinned and handsome as all outdoors. He was manner able, considerate and very smart as well. The deal my mom made with me was that I could date but not have sex and that she would go where we go and monitor our relationship closely because she wanted to ensure goodness for me. Jeremy loved taking us out riding for joy. We would go out to eat and just enjoy the day or night out riding. Because Jeremy was such a good mannered boy, my mom became comfortable and allowed us to be alone two years later which gave Jeremy and I the opportunity to become sexually active with each other. Shelly was now sixteen, with a boyfriend and sexually active. The relationship continued to be well until my eleventh grade year and I found that Jeremy had dropped out of school and not gotten his education. My mom and I encouraged Jeremy to go to Job Corps along with my brother Robert who was around the same age as Jeremy to try and further his education. Jeremy agreed, therefore, my brother and boyfriend were off to Tuskegee to do their thing as I insured I love for Jeremy and he did the same in return. As time passed with me and Jeremy being apart, my brother was bringing report that not only had Jeremy been mistreating him but he was also cheating on me with all types of females, nasty ones at that. Being that Robert would only report after him and Jeremy had fallouts, Jeremy would always tell me that was the reason Robert was making those accusations, claiming his innocence. I already knew there was a possibility that the cheating could be true because Jeremy was no saint while he was near me. He had been caught sleeping with the ex-girlfriend but claimed it was over and done. I was a fool in love but starting to veer in the direction of getting myself another man; made a huge wrong move. I ended up in meeting in school this guy by the name of Ivan. Ivan and I were the same age and he seems to be a good hearted fellow with wonderful respect and manners. I actually started to see this guy and fell in love. Ivan and I ended in going to the same vocational school and this is where things got crazy. Ivan and I started to date real hot and heavy, so much that Ivan started taking his mother's vehicle in the middle of the night to come and see me. He was sneaking through my bedroom window and I at this time didn't feel anything wrong with it. Ivan and I were in love, he had his own job and was a very responsible guy; would buy me anything I asked for and we vowed to be together forever. I was feeling bad about having Jeremy and decided to tell Ivan about him and tell Jeremy that I no longer wanted to be with him.

The Fatal Twist

Ivan and I had decided that one more night would be spent with him coming through my window as I would now introduce him to everybody and make things official. Ivan came down that night at 2:00 am in the morning and we made what we called sweet passionate love and declared our lives to each other and swore that all would be out in the open. We had decided to take a joy ride in Ivan mother's car that night as well. Ivan help me get in and out of my bedroom window with no problems but the kicker came as my sister Tessa noticed Ivan's car outside of the house and sneaked into our parents' room to tell that I had Ivan in the room. As I quickly put close on and Ivan hide under the bed while my parents knocked at my closed room door, my heart was beating immensely. I just knew I was caught and everything would come crumbling down. Even though I was doing something so wrong, one of God's angels was with me. My father was yelling as I opened my bedroom door, "Who you got in that room, I got my gun and I am going to kill whoever it is." My door comes open and my father states; "I can smell sex all over the room, "I know somebody up in here" and I was scared to death but I held it together and stated no one was in my room. I even told my parents they could look around. I had held a lie about being raped, what was one more lie, I was thinking. I could not let them catch Ivan in my room because he was special to me. Being with Ivan was finally something and he was someone I was proud to have in my life, I wanted to make it right. My mom had peeked out a pair of shoes at the foot of the bed which belong to Ivan but I confessed that they belong to Jeremy and I had them a while. My parents finally gave in but told me to leave the bedroom door open as everyone went back to sleep and Ivan eased from under the bed. How he got out without his shoes of course was by me acting as if she had to go to the bathroom and closing the door slightly to allow Ivan to ease out of the window. That same morning Ivan never made it home and the morning came as one of Ivan's brother called me to see what was going on. I was shocked to find Ivan was getting help from this brother to take his mother's car nightly to see me. Because I didn't know at first, thinking everything to be untrue, told the brother I hadn't seen Ivan. It finally came to pass that Ivan had an accident in his mother's car after leaving my house. Not knowing the whole detail of everything and clueless to what Ivan was experiencing, I was keeping my promise to him to get rid of Jeremy; for the report of him was never good anyways. When Jeremy called that day, I told him that it was over and that I was moving on with Ivan. Jeremy was all dramatic and told me that I couldn't quit him and that he was coming home, declaring we were going to be together. Jeremy was my least concern and I professed that our relationship was done. I then sought to call Ivan and let him know everything, finding he was truly hospitalized and almost lost his life. He had lain unconscious in a pond of water for hours after running off the road to falling asleep at the wheel. I was shocked, hurt and felt it was my entire fault. I told Ivan that I wanted to be with him and had done all that I needed to do for us to be together and our relationship was in the making.

It was two days later that Jeremy showed up like he said and hell broke loose. Jeremy came and that's when I found that Ivan and Jeremy were cousins and he convinced me that Ivan only wanted me because he knew I was with him. Jeremy sat in my mother's house as my parents were gone shopping and put a gun to my head and told me that if I didn't call Ivan and tell him that the relationship was over that he would kill me. Not knowing what to do, I did as he said and Jeremy would not give me room to breathe that day. He stayed over all day and half of the night convincing me that Ivan was bad business and that Ivan had been telling the neighborhood boys about me; stating Ivan was giving me a bad reputation. He claimed others had told him that Ivan had herpes and that he probably had given it to me. Jeremy claimed Ivan was sleeping with all the nasty neighborhood females and the list of accusations go on and on. Jeremy turned out to be a crazy, controlling, cheating, manipulating maniac whom I got stuck with for two more years. The love that Ivan and I shared went astray when Ivan's father forbids him to talk with me. Jeremy made sure to take advantage of the situation. Something that was once a great love affair ended with a tragic result of deceit, guilt and distrust on Ivan's and my part. As time passed and I was stuck with Jeremy, I found all that my brother had proclaimed was coming to pass. Jeremy got so bold with his cheating and controlling ways it came out that he had been having relationships with my cousins, friends and anyone else that would let him as he play innocent causing all kind of trouble to my heart and mind. In high school I was hated by my own kinfolk who went out of their way to ruin the relationship I had with Jeremy because he was so open. He used this as the excuse to get me to consider being intimate with him against my mother's will and before appropriate time; claiming he had needs and had to get it somewhere while he was trying to respect my wishes because he loved me. I was young and naïve, therefore allowing Jeremy to disgrace me. The first incident was with my cousin Mary and Rosanna; they went to his house as Mary threw herself at him and took pictures and everything as she sat in his lap, just too have proof and bring back evidence of the report. Mary's hate towards me came from the devil using her to try and hurt me mentally because I loved Jeremy and Mary was jealous of little me. God was trying to show me who Jeremy was and it didn't stop there. Prom day, I caught him and another cousin together at the auto parts store. Veronica was her name and she was another who just wanted to see me unhappy and have what I had. Veronica had a boyfriend at the time and he wanted to try and even up the score by calling me and telling me everything that happen while asking me to get with him, A LIE! The cousins were the last as God tried to remove this guy from my life. He started messing with one of my classmates from high school after I moved to Tuscaloosa, Alabama with him. Emotionally I was torn to pieces. The trouble I experienced with what I realized was infatuation instead of love with was unbearable. Not only did this boy treat me like the naïve little girl I was but he almost made me kill myself. Knowing that I had nothing special anymore to offer a good man, I allowed myself to be controlled, cheated on, mentally abused and emotionally scared. I was giving my sex away because it was not a big deal to save myself as I had already been defiled. I had gotten so fed up with my relationship with Jeremy and tired of trying to throw stone of hurt for hurt that I actually took eighteen Tylenol pills one day. All I could think about was how miserable I was with him and how I had let my mother, my family and Ivan down; with things being so out of order. I was feeling as if I had let her mother down again and didn't need to live anymore. It was one pill for everyday that I lived and I laid on the couch in wait to just die and nobody knew. God had to be with me because as I lay there sick on the stomach all I did was regurgitate those pills and water, not needing to go to the doctor or anything. Guess who shows up after that only to make me feel even more bad and angry, yes, Jeremy. After realizing God saw fit to spare my life, I grew a backbone and continued about another few months with Jeremy until I went to the doctor and found I had Chlamydia. I knew Jeremy had been a cheater and if he would give me this disease, there was more to come if I keep on with him; he would ruin her life. Finally I got my parents involved and Jeremy was made to stay away. I finally got rid of Jeremy and decided to try and find Ivan to see if we could rekindle our love for it had seem to be a strong one; it was just wrong at the wrong time. Ivan by this time had moved to Birmingham, Alabama, as we were finished high school and to my knowledge Ivan was single. I called to Ivan's house in hopes his family would provide me information to speak with him. I was blessed and spoke with the brother, who was helping him to be with me, although he was hesitant, he gave me contact information for Ivan. It was not easy to get the information from Ivan's brother as he was afraid I would hurt Ivan again. I made a promise to Ivan's brother that all was different this time around. When I called Ivan, he was overjoyed and I was finally feeling like I was on the right track with my heart. Ivan came down that night to visit me and of course as usual we shared a passionate kiss and rekindled our love. It was as if the relationship had never ended and we were picking up right where we left off. Unbeknownst to my knowledge, Ivan didn't trust me at all and used that to his advantage. Ivan used what happen in the past to keep me in the foolish ring. I had felt guilty about the whole incident and wanted to repair all of the damage I felt I had caused Ivan all those years. Ivan would come home and spend a day or two, have sex with me and leave. Out of that hold time he would visit, he would spend less than an hour with me; deceit was starting to add up. Ivan asked me to buy him gifts to prove my love and even placing money in his bank account for him. I had a job so it was no big deal and if this is what I had to do to get back into his good graces then it was done. The problem came when Ivan decided he would bring me up for a weekend visit as he also worked that weekend. I was left alone at his house that he shared with other friends and found tons and tons of female numbers and letters from this girl whom Ivan claimed he never had any dealings with. See here's the problem, this female name Yvonne that I attended high school with during the time Ivan and I had proclaimed our love was going around telling people that she and Ivan were having a relationship back then as well. Yvonne claimed that night that Ivan had the accident that almost killed him, he had just left her house; which means, Ivan left me and went to Yvonne for a couple of hours. I never believed that story but now as I see and read these letters upon letters that he has in his drawer from her, I can believe it all to be true. As I read through letters upon letters my heart was torn because Yvonne was describing encounter after encounter that the two of them had ever had and how she loved him so much that she followed him to the same city and state. Not really knowing how to feel or what to do, I finished the weekend off with Ivan but decided since he was not who I believed him to be that I would move forward and give Ivan his space. Ivan and I continued our distant relationship but I was no longer open and available for him when he would just pop up in town and expect me to come running. I had begun to date someone else and I was having fun. The kicker came when Ivan called himself professing to me that he wanted to spend the rest of his life with me and that he loved me only. He told me about this friend girl he had and that nothing was going on but he needed to be open and honest and get the truth out about what had been going on with him. Well, one day when I called up to Ivan after all that confessing and truth giving, a female answered his phone. It was Retina, the female friend Ivan had told me about, being naïve, I greeted Retina and Retina in return greeted me. Ivan had told Retina all about me except for the fact that I was supposed to be his girlfriend. As I asked for Ivan and where he was, Retina responded with saying she was laying in the bed right beside him; my mouth drops open and things are never the same. I told Retina to put Ivan on the phone and he answered as if I was not on the line. "Hello, Hello", Ivan says as I was trying to ask him about the Retina situation. Ivan then tells Retina, "Hang up the phone, there's no one on the line" and the line goes dead. I was so over and done with Ivan. It didn't even take three minutes but my phone was ringing only for it to be Ivan on the other end confessing and telling me he was sorry and never meant to hurt me. Ivan claimed Retina was just a spare to keep him from getting hurt by me. He claims because I didn't move to Birmingham with him and be with him that he had to have someone there and that he didn't trust me not to break his heart and that everything was all a big mistake but Ivan kept telling me he loved me and wanted me. Ivan was so caught in his mess that I firmly told him I was done. Ivan came in town the next day to try and convince me that our love could be what we always wanted it to be. Ivan swore he would make me fall completely in love and in trust with him again but I wasn't having it. Ivan came down to my job to try and convince me to love him. He pleaded arrogantly, with me knowing he didn't mean any of what he was saying. I soon came to find that Ivan didn't want me but just didn't want anybody else to have me either. He was everything Jeremy had claimed with added injuries. He was no better than Jeremy and now I had to get over both of them. That was it, I had found my release, did all I could do and the guilt was no longer on me for what happened when Ivan and I were teenagers. I had some real issues going on that I could not explain and was experiencing because of my virginity being taken and feeling like I wasn't truly deserving of anyone as well as accepting anybody into my life. It took my years to get over Ivan. I would still call him on his birthday, during the holidays and any day I knew was special to him because I truly loved him. Throughout that time I even sent prayer up to have the chance to lay with him just one more time and it was answered. We met and made love to Maxwell song, "Fortunate!" God had allowed that moment and time and I was keeping my promise to God to get over him and that was it. After being raped and getting into one bad relationship after another, and not knowing who to trust or love, I became a hot mess through the years ranging from 1989 through 2001. I gained so many different aspects of myself, went through so much hell, had so many different boys and never found true Godly love with any of them. I had gotten so defiled in my mind that I began to use sex as a weapon for what I wanted or felt I needed. Being that I was a fair skinned female with long pretty hair and eyes with a size coca cola bottle shape, I was every man's dream where I lived because that image was gorgeous. I got so evil in my heart that I was treating men like they treat women with the one night stands, seeking out a man to just have a sexual relationship, taking men's money or making them fall in love with me and then disappearing. I was something to be reckoned with as I was meeting men offline and everything; living a very dangerous lifestyle. It wasn't until one night as I was dating this guy who was crazy and I mean crazy because he was receiving disability benefits. Dealing with him made me turn my life around. My grandmother was actually visiting over at my mom and dad's house and she had stayed for four days and nights there. My boyfriend had also gotten kicked out of his mom house so my mom allowed me and my boyfriend to stay in my room, because there were bunk beds and forbid us to be having sex in her house. In trying to be respectful of my mother's wishes, I did just what she said. My grandmother was there and she was a very religious woman, therefore I surely dare not to disrespect. As I did all I could do to keep my promise of not sleeping around in my mother's house, this crazy boyfriend starting to accuse me of sleeping with someone and that was the reason I wasn't worried about giving him any. Let me remind you that for three days straight, I mean day and night; my grandmother had been praying and wouldn't let up. I at this time was also deciding to change my life around and try to find God as I had always had the teachings and upbringing but didn't have that personal relationship I was now seeking. Me and this boyfriend began to verbally and physically fight and during that time on the last and third night in which my grandmother was praying and I decided right then and there that my craziness was over. I would no longer belittle myself and defile my body any longer; that the next man who touched me would marry me and that guy was made to leave and never return again. He kept following me around and trying to come to my job a couple of days but after that God made him disappear. This is where I realized my grandmother must have been praying for me because finally I felt the need to get myself in the right track of life.

Chapter 4

A New Time in Life

Time went on and I keep to myself, got into school and by this time it was a new year, 2001. This year was a new transition for me and I was going to make it happen. I ended up in getting married that year after dating for six months after all I had known this guy all of my life, his parents, kinfolk and everything else. He also knew these same things about me so what more was there left to do, nothing but as the scripture say, "Better to marry than to burn!" Little did I know that I would have a ruff few years with that marriage ending in a divorce only to have to gather myself and find myself right back where I started?

In my marriage I experienced some of the most horrifying things ever. Within the first year of my marriage my husband was using my cell phone to call back call his ex girlfriend. When I confronted him and asked where had I went wrong; why he doesn't love me as he should, Jamal answered by asking me, "why didn't I love herself?" I had to think about that because of the things I was allowing into my life. God allowed the devil to present me with a question that would haunt me for the next four years of my and Jamal's marriage. I was married to a thug, a cheat and a baby boy. As I called myself growing into a woman and trying to invent a man to come along with me, I experienced pure hell. I remember how I got physically punched in the face by my husband because he thought I was talking to other men. I could not even attempt to look at another man for I was accused of having a relationship with him. Jamal went as far as to physically abuse me to the point of me having to call the cops just to make him go away. The final straw of disrespect came when Jamal stayed out all night and would be out with other women. I actually caught him trying to buy a hotel room for him another female. I was at my lowest with this marriage as I keep reading my bible and asking God to take over because I was trying to stay on God's will for my life. I experienced five years of hell until I decided enough was enough and leave so much that I had to venture into a different state to renew my heart and mind.

I was so sure all could change that I went for the church man, he didn't work, military man, he didn't work, I had your modeling man, when he didn't work, I went for the business man, he didn't work, and I ended up with the pimp with a hidden crack habit. One of the sweetest, smooth talking pimps I could have ever met in my life. I will call him Notorious, for he sent a whirling winding into my life that almost had me living on the streets which is where he wanted me ,"BUT GOD!" Notorious came to me at a time where I was not looking to be into a serious relationship, and he made sure to take advantage of the moment. He was tall, pecan toned in skin color, light brown eyes, low hair cut, the most pretty white teeth you have ever seen in your life, always neatly dressed from his head down to his toes. Notorious was straight out of male modeling magazine. He was fit from head to toe and my nose was wide open as he talked about having a personal relationship with God, seeking to become a model, had the gift of reading people and was seeking to go higher in life; one of his goals, being a male model. Not knowing this dude was a previous cracked out vagabond, who had been hospitalized for overdosing as he shot up, with no telling to what diseases hide underneath his perfectly fit physique body, he was bipolar, schizophrenic and known for seducing woman to move with him to another city, having them to pawn and sell everything they own to leave them low and dry in the end. He got me real good as I sold the home I lived in, move to a different state with the apartment in my name, loan money for an extra car for him to drive with no license and he had plans to live off me until I was on the streets myself. Notorious and I lived in a two bedroom apartment, where I struggled to pay the rent and gain long-term employment which almost had me on the street. My whole world can crumbling in with this guy as he mentally controlled everything I did and tried to control my money and how I spent it. Notorious even got me into bringing another female into the house claiming she was going to uphold his parts of the bill and he was taking her money and cracking it up. God surely had me covered because I never ended up on the street nor did I have to sale my body like Notorious was trying to push me to do to survive. That relationship, whatever one would want to call it, truly made me think twice about picking a man because of his looks. He use to tell me he had bookies and needed money but being he would laugh it off, I thought he was joking. I did not know this guy was a crack head because he would leave the house usually with a bottle of brown liquor in the brown bag and come back an hour later all wild and crazy but claiming it to be the liquor. He had once had the conversation with me that all a crack head had to do to keep himself up was eat before he go and smoke or shoot up his crack, exercise and buy some whitening tooth formula for his teeth and no one would tell the difference but I just thought it was random conversation until I experienced firsthand with him. This was the last and final straw as he had gotten me to pawn all my movies, jewelry, desktop computer and more only to bring another female in who was suppose to help but didn't plus he brought a second female in who had just gotten out of jail for writing bad checks and I was shooting fire from my nostrils. The week that I allowed her to stay there turned into an ugly situation that caused me to call the cops. I got tired of him meeting my company at the door with a bat while he brought strays in. One day I got up the nerve and called the cops on him to make him leave, not knowing that if he had lived over 30 days or had clothes at my spot I could not just put him out. He and that female in front of the police made this lie about all of us being in a threesome relationship and I was mad about him choosing her. Guess which cop believed the story and told me to shut my mouth as I was trying to disprove their lie? It was the fat, manly looking, bull-dagger officer. This is where I looked Notorious in the eyes and made him a promise right there with the cops standing, that he would never get the opportunity to live in another home I lay my head in and once I got him out; he better not show his face again. He knew that I meant every word I said and I went and got the eviction notice. This clown had to go and I did what was necessary to ensure his leave. I took him back where I got him and dropped him off; yep, the state where we had moved from, and five hours away. After Notorious was gone, I found a piece of crack on the bedroom floor he slept in.

The Ultimate Life Changer

I was being careful after this dreadful move. I was trying to be careful of my next move and relationship only to end up with a hustler who would change my life forever. Kavarius was his name! He had told me he could change my life and he didn't lie. Kavarius professed he had been a rap artist in the early 2000 and use to be a friend with one of the well known rap artist in the "A!" He made claims that he and the well known rap artist had a falling out over a female and he was just dumped off. Kavarius seemed to become very sensitive and angry when he would see a video or hear any music from the well known artist. He would often tell me the stories on the wild adventures he experienced while in the rap game and entertainment business, very interesting I must admit. He showed me the cd's and let me listen to the music that he and this well known artist had created. He was in a group that the well known artist had created as well during that time. When I met him he was hustling to live but he had a great hustle for he was still dressing neat, smelling good, looking good and trying to restart his career. This is where

I thought my life had turned around for the best until I encountered all the lies he told, the hustling he was doing right to me and the loop he was placing me in. I spent nine months trying to untangle the web Kavarius had placed me in because I was thirty, naïve and gullible. Here's the story:

Loving With No Return

It started out as a simple meet of page words and no face on Blackplanet.com. He stated he was twenty-five and his interest seems so real. I myself was thirty at the time so twenty-five not a bad age at all, as long as he keeps asking me key seem of interest questions. We started to have conversation day after day, long lengths of time. I was really feeling him. He started to come by at 4:00 in the morning but it was nothing sexual about his visits. He would lie beside me and cuddle. O my, everything I had ever dreamed. He told me he was the Ceo of his own Company, fallen but up and coming rap artist with a vision that would change the street prospective. So you know I am in awe, I can see that he definitely has the potential. Then I get the seven pink roses on the door step, the flowers came at least three times and two cards. He's really interested, o my. He was the one; he wanted to know who I was, what were my past hurt, present expectations, and my future needs and wants. He tells me that my dream of having a child will come, that he only has one daughter and still has the dream of a son.

Time passes, as we continue to go out on dinner dates, spend time together, he continued to tell me his dreams, hopes, and wishes, but then I noticed everything was turning out to be iffy. He was more so complaining the putting forth action to make a life for himself and I through means of his own. He wanted me to obtain health insurance for him, rent out cars for him to drive weekly and buy the time he was spending with me. He would say He was missing out on money coming to see me. Soon all things came to past after I became pregnant for him. He use to be friends with a well known rap artist that promised him they would make it to the top together. The man in my life was a fallen rap artist who never made it all the way to the top but still tried to live the life and dream by any means. He was a Street Pharmacists, twenty-three years old, and not wanting any kids other than the daughter he had, whom in nine months of dating, I never met. After seeing pictures of her and hearing him talk about her so much, I could tell he loved her, but what about me?

I found out I had been lied to about who he was altogether after becoming pregnant with his firm decision of abortion. God blocked that though. He took the baby at eight weeks instead. I didn't find out the baby had passed until I had my accident. I walked out of that accident without a scratch because God had previously prepared for my life. As I lay baffled on the emergency room bed after being told my child was dead, I contacted my unborn child's father. He didn't care, he never came to the hospital when called nor did he come to the house to take care of me after having to have surgery to remove the child, but still he claimed he loved me. I was loving this man with no return. It took me nine months of questions, assumptions, wondering, holding on, and trying to find ways to not accept what I already knew from the moment of meeting him. He was not for me and I was loving with no return...

Beautiful Beginning

How everything began, let's head back to July 25, 2007, where I was so desperate in need of love. Yes, I admit it, I was seeking real true love, and therefore I became open to the first men who seem to be genuine. A lot of us make this mistake. Therefore, I was online and I was going through page after page looking to see if I could find someone smart enough, handsome enough, godly enough, and most of all, real enough to come into my world. After all, I had just gotten upon my feet by six months in the game since moving to Georgia. I didn't need someone who was going to bring me right back to where I just started from even if I was desperate for love. I needed that man to hold equal partnership. I needed him to bring something to the table as well as myself.

I am online and becoming very discouraged until this one particular message comes through at 7:29 pm," You look good Ms. Lady." That was different and this was the first time I had heard someone use that phrase, therefore I go and look at the page which had no picture but his writing seemed so real and straight forward. I give thought to hearing what he has to say. His page read, "what's up too all the women who are on BP! I appreciate you stopping by my page to see what I got to offer. As you can see I'm Stay-Focused because that's all I try to do every day, stay-focused! No I don't have a picture on my page or some of that stupid stuff my so called competition be putting on their page, but it is no problem to send you one. I do me and I feel like I don't need to show or even tell what it is I got or how I live, if you are a real woman like you suppose to be forget how many times you say it, you will respect it! I think way different from my competitors; I am a person who is going somewhere so therefore I try to surround myself around positive people. I stay too myself and I am independent. Now I know you like "all these niggs say the same thing" and u are right, I absolutely agree but here is where you try to treat the situation like a pair of dice, go on and roll'em baby. This '07 baby, we made it, stay focused and beautiful inside and out. Don't let anybody tell you different. Whatever any of you women want to talk about feel free to drop a note, everybody needs someone to talk to, even you women who got a man. It doesn't matter as long as you are a real person! Halla at me if you invest, I am an investor.

Now, with looking back on what he said in his message, it was real and had I been put up on game, I would have been able to point out the key answers to my questions of why I loving with no return. If you look closely to what he wrote, it was evident that this man was a gambler with life and relationships, key quote, "Now I know u like all these niggs say the same thing" and you are right, I absolutely agree but here is where you try to treat the situation like a pair of dice, go on and roll'em baby." In reading back as well, another key answer to knowing this man was not ready to be committed, "everybody need someone to talk to, even you women who got a man. It doesn't matter as long as you are a real person!" Third quote to tell he was in the game of using if you gave him the chance,"Halla at me if you invest, I am an investor." These were three key signs that stuck out to tell me to stay away but I chose to ignore. I could go all day on pointers in his personal note that will give you 100% knowledge of things I should have known. If my eyes and ears had been open instead of my lonely heart, I would have avoided this whole situation which has cost me so much.

Here is where I knock my own self in the head. I then write back and let him know I was interested and wanted that picture he said he could give. He writes back and says, "Maybe we can get to know each other better if possible. I am a very respectful man who has a daughter, she is 4 years old. I am not on here looking for no woman or women to try and do something with, just a friend who can understand me as a person. If interested halla at me!! Stay cute!"

That was the winning note but had I had my game radar up, I would have seen all these signs. All I had to do was look and listen but I ignored the key answers. The way he truly got in was when he asked, "Do you like to eat? I appreciate you getting back to me. I like to site see and do things that make me happy like a movie or the park to get a peace of mind. If I ever have time to do that!! What about you? Do you like to read? What interest you?" This was the kicker;

he was fattening and buttering me up, all at the same time. I then I write, do I like to eat??? Did you see the thickness on my page? I love to eat, good quality food. I like the movies and walks in the park. I will write poetry in a minute or read books. We might end in being real good friends after all. Good conversation and no pressure is what interest me. He got me now, and finally he writes, "ok sounds good!" Maybe in due time we can grab something to eat of course after the whole process of meeting each other is over. I would love to be a good friend of yours, if you allow me to be. Are you the only one or do you have brothers/sisters? Who do you admire? If it could be one place where you could go, where would it be and what would you do?" There it is, He's all up in my business, getting all my info, and I let him because I responded with giving him my number and that's how we became partners.

He calls and we talk for hours over the phone, found out he was a Leo, same sign as my deceased mom, whom was a great woman. She was my best friend. So you know this gave him even more open room to get in. I thought his character would be the same or similar to hers. To be truthful, he wasn't a bad guy; he was just bad for me because of the lifestyle he was living. He made had some mistakes that caused him such embarrassment that he chose to lie about it instead of speaking the truth and moving forward in his life without deceit.

First Meeting

Finally, we get to the part of the first meet and as I stated earlier it was at 4:00 am in the morning; reminder that there was nothing sexual at all about that meeting though. He came over for a few minutes and dipped before sun break. I should have known a lot of things that aren't seen at night can be seen during the day. So whenever he came to see me starting out would be at the a.m. hours of the night before day break. I was starting to feel odd and beginning to ask if he was a vampire or something because he only comes out at night. You know this is Atlanta, Georgia and they have some everything going on here. I then started to think maybe he was an upcoming rap artist or something and was hiding from his fans. A girl can dream that she meeting a star can't she? He was always dressed well and smelled so good. Finally, I get up enough courage to ask why I couldn't see him during the day. He responded with, "It is hard for me to get through with my work, which takes me into the a.m. hours. I told you I don't have a lot of dating time." Wait, I thought we were just friends. Hmmm, I am starting to think and the next morning I get a phone call from him telling me to open my door. I am thinking he decided to step up and let me see him during the day, therefore, I open the door and no one is there. I then look down and upon my door step lay roses, Awe! He bought seven pink roses, how thoughtful. Boy, he knows how to get a girl; he really knows what to do. I got the pink roses and thanked him for them and while he and I were still over the phone he asked if I knew what it meant for a man to give a woman pink roses. I am from Alabama, no idea! He giggles and advised me to go search around online and it will tell me everything. In my eyes this was romantic; in his, he got my country butt. We keep it moving though as I look around on line to find what being given pink roses meant and I find; light pink roses are associated with gentleness and admiration, and can also be used as an expression of fondness and sympathy, as well as friendship. Okay, so he really got game but now I am loving it even more; never had a man do this before. Kavarius or Mr. Stay Focused and I begin to have a very nice friendship which quickly turned into something more. I remember how he first came over during the day and I was shocked. It's funny how I never paid any attention to what he drove over to my apartment, because I would always be in the bed and too sleepy to try and look. So the first day he told me to get ready and he would see me shortly to take me out to dinner; it was exciting. He showed up in this 2007 dodge that was brand new and shiny. I am thinking o'hell is this really a man I am messing with; he got money. Yes! Finally a man with his own; I was surely rolling the dice and baby they had rolled on all sevens; I am thinking he's a winner. I am just as nervous as I want to be. My stomach was turning flips inside out to see him in the day light, ride in this fancy car and be alongside such a handsome man; yes momma I think I found him, I was thinking. He took me to a Mexican restaurant to try some different foods other than the regular country food I knew; sadly it didn't turn out well so he got me some McDonalds. We hung out the whole day and he kept me laughing and engaged. He was cool and he was different and that is what made me fall in love. Yes I said it. As we continued to date, I found myself more and more nervous every time he looked at me, touched me or anything. I fell for him real fast when I kept trying not to. I went to my best friend and asked if I should stop everything before it got started and she paraded me to go with what I was feeling; boy what was I thinking.

In the Relationship

We began to spend a lot more time together after that first meeting and would always seem to be engaged in each other much. Mr. Stay Focused was very fun-loving and easy to be around. He was smart, non-judgmental and most of all; real. He was what I felt I needed. He was getting in very good with a sister and yet we had not had any sex. I got the opportunity to share what I thought was his 26th birthday but was actually his 24th birthday with him because of all the tangled lies he feed me. I bought him a money greeting card and placed a fifty dollar bill in it; I should have known to him that was measly money but I am from Alabama and that is a lot; plus it is the thought that counts. I notice that he never took the card with him but he did take the money, okay! He told me that he wanted me to keep the card with me because his life was so busy and he is moving around a lot that it may get lost therefore he wanted to make sure it was kept. Damn, he's married is the thought that came to my mind but I had to give him a chance to prove me wrong and he did. He wasn't a married man; it was a lot more complicated than that. Everything was on the up and up and one night I got a little tipsy off some wine. I called him up and he was acting as if he was surprised to hear that I drank a little and I wanted him to come by. It had been a year since sex and I was horny. He was a good-looking man and we had played around plenty with touching, therefore I was ready. He came over that September 3rd night and we got loose. He kept asking me if I was sure and if I would have any regrets. I should have paused and thought about what he was saying but instead I answered; I'm sure, no regrets!!!! I wanted him and he felt good as well as smelt good. Where I thought he was being considerate of me, it was really him trying to warn me about what I was about to get into. I am getting chills as I write the story about that night. I had never felt so sexually satisfied in my life; that loving was good and he knew just what to do with it and how. Every inch that he placed inside of me, along with every thrust carried me out of this world. He held me tight as we rhythmically moved with each other; it was as if I was a young school girl in love for the very first time. He sent my swinging from the ceiling that night and it was over. I knew why I was afraid of him, he had that good love but that wasn't all of it.

As our sexual appetites increased, I began to ask more questions into who he was. I wanted to know the man I was dealing with as well as giving all my sex too. He was receiving my soul, my mind and heart. We would often have intimate conversations and spent lots of time together although it all came with an unknown catch. I got into braiding his hair; renting his luxury vehicles and watching him become over dramatic about everything. See, becoming intimate with him meant he was an investor and I was investing. The friends with benefit played its role so perfectly in this deal. Little did I know in the beginning but I was dealing with a queen. Yes I said it and I said it loud and clear! An over-grown dramatized queen of a man he was I say. We had a lovely relationship that was filled with friendship, sex and bought love until I became pregnant. Thank God for that pregnancy and miscarriage because this is where I found out whom I was truly dealing with. His over exaggerated acting helped me to find out I was pregnant. He had come over falling all out stating he was feeling very sick. He was trying to make himself regurgitate and everything. He had a pregnancy test with him when he came over; therefore the man knew he had knocked me up. He told me I was going to have to abort and this is where his madness came in. He knew I was against abortion but because of the life he was living he didn't want me to have his child. He wanted to continue having sex, have me renting his luxury vehicles as he pretends to love me and respect me but I could not have his child. While he made me feel really good; he made me feel very bad in the same sense. He was the type who could disrespect you but make you think he's respecting you at the same time. It is a very sore subject so I will leave that one alone although things did not end after I went through the miscarriage ordeal and finding out how he really felt about the entire situation. After I found out all of the lies and he no longer played Mr. Perfect anymore, so many things began to come to a head. Why I didn't just let go after that, I could not tell. Yes I can, it was that "bunker busting loving" that man put on me. Although he turned out to be years younger than he had first told me and a non committer, I still wanted what he was able to offer; sex, laughter, time, conversation and friendship. I wanted to give him a chance to make it right. He was romantic and I loved him; it's hard to let that go. I was more watchful but I still cared for him. Our relationship began to take on some sadistic moments.

It All Falls Down

When I finally decided I was going to be watchful he came over crying and hollering like a girl. He was putting on a show for me until I turned and saw him watching his own self in the mirror squeezing tears from his eyes. He felt ashamed and sat on my bathroom toilet seat in the dark. He proceeded to declare his undying love towards what I provided that no one else did. He was in love with my person, my carefulness, my unconditional love and he didn't want to lose me. My best friend was over that day and he claimed that he thought she had persuaded me against him. I told him, he did that all by himself but as I saw that he wanted to at least keep a loving friendship, therefore, I decided to offer that. During the end time of our relationship things got really crazy and so much began to unravel. Not only did we get stuck into this crazy friendship but we also continued this attachment of not wanting each other to be in a relationship with no one else. Mr. Stay-Focused somehow started to become unfocused as I began to find out his true person. I use to watch this man cry to a point of sadistic behavior every time he saw the rap artist he claimed he was partners with back in his beginning to be famous days. He would always give the story about how this guy left him behind as he got big and famous. He talked and cried so much about the situation that I started flicking off the Atlanta based rap artist. I was mad at him because he was mad at him, just crazy. He would always get into the stories about life as an artist and tell adventurous stories about the ones he got to spend time with and hang around. If this is what the business was, I know I wanted no parts of that. At one point in my life I wanted to be a singer.

I was so caught up in this man that I could not see the obvious. We once took a stroll through Lenox mall and while I thought all eyes were on us it was really on the bank deposit envelope he was twirling around in his hands, he knew how to get attention. I remember starting to have thoughts that maybe I was dealing with a bisexual man; after all, he was living the street life. He was at my apartment one day and he received a phone call from a man that you could hear clearly was a homosexual male. He was asking if he was coming over to get high with him and he would cook for him. After that phone call you know I was on him. He claimed that the guy was a client. So I go and say; "what kind of client is this? You selling what and I hope it's not your sex." He laughed me off and claimed it was the substance. Clearly that was not the end to my thinking, of course now I am playing detective and start to watch what he do and say. It all boiled down to us going out to eat and three drag-queens staring him down to him calling me and telling me his baby mama had called him out. What real man without practicing some kind of homosexual behavior would tell his woman that his baby momma said he needed to stop selling himself to white whores and giving up booty to men for money? I was dealing with a "trade" as they call them boys now days. No wonder he would cry over the Atlanta rap artist, he was either his groupie or in love with him. It's no wonder that he wanted to put some steel in him and knew his every move. Like I said, things were crazy and as I think back to the night we first made love and he asked if it was what I really wanted and if I would have any regrets, I realize why now. He knew all of the things he was into and he knew I wouldn't be acceptable to the man he truly was. For a second he thought that if he fitted it all just right I would never find out but just in case I did, he could always revert to saying, "I asked if you were sure and if you would have any regrets!" Well, so the world will know, I don't regret and I was sure! It was all an experience and I had to learn. It was my lesson. No Mistake, No Experience, No Lesson Learned. I loved with no return.

After that hot mess of a relationship I decided this time for real and because of all the things life had dealt me that I was going to do better about myself. I was finally going to answer that question my ex-husband had asked in the first year of our marriage, "Why didn't I love myself?" I started to go through all of the things that had happened to me from day one of my life. I saw how God had brought me through and kept angels camped around me to save and spare my life. I saw how I was still blessed although I was doing nothing that was good and made a vow to change my own life forever. I began to sit back, think and write about all of my failures to find where I went wrong and answer that one big question, "Why didn't I love myself?"

Chapter 5

Soul Ties

This in-depth moment of thinking lead Shelly to write “Soul Ties.” The write-up: Many people wonder why there are so many relationships that keep going wrong and cannot be worked out. Throughout my story as a witness to what I have named "Soul Ties," I will give you the answer that you need. I am sure it will answer many questions to why there are so many personality crashes and misunderstandings in relationships that end in failure. Throughout my life; I have learned, seen, witnessed, and heard about the relationships that fail or the past keeping an individual man or woman from gracefully finding real and true love. Now days, many of us find ourselves going from partner to partner only to gain spirits that tie us to each man or woman we lay down with and for many, let within our heart and minds.

In living these 33 years, I have come to realize about 3 years ago something that is very real and true. Guess what ladies and gentlemen? Each time we lay down to have sex; we spiritually tie our self with that person whom we lay with. "How can I dare say such a thing; you ask? Here's my story and examples of the spiritual ties and past relationships keeping you bounded. We have several spirits: to name a few; there is love, hate, disgust, confusion, misunderstanding, manipulation, the spirit of destroy, jealousy and etc.

For many years, even with knowing God and be a Christian woman, I allowed some spiritual ties. I grew up in the church and never imagined how confused the spiritual ties made me. My first spiritual tie began at thirteen when I was raped which was the first taking of my soul, the second, at sixteen years of age where I was in my first relationship and I loved him so I thought, it was just infatuation that turned to hate once the relationship was over. It was because of everything he did to me while I was infatuated with him. He slept with other females; such as family members, friends and high school classmates. Every time I lay with him before and after I became tied spiritually. He was putting jealousy, hurt, pain, destroy and all kinds of spirits inside of me. Even after leaving him at age nineteen, I was still tied to him and what he did to me just carried over to the next man, the next man and the next. That's how many of us allow the past to stain our future.

When you lay with someone and they are confused, then guess what you are left with when they leave or you leave them, that's right confusion. Then you call yourself getting involved with someone else only to find they are misunderstanding and hateful. So now guess what you have; confusion, misunderstanding and hate. The ties continue and continue until you realize and decide it must stop here and now. Imagine thirty years of all these ties building up and accumulating. I was something to be reckoned with and many men and women are the same.

What I ask is that before you tie yourself spiritually to another man or woman, make sure it's ordained by God and their past ties isn't in their future. Lose yourself of those spirits that keep you confused, lonely, hurt, resentful, painful, full of hate, full of destruction and more. Starting today, don't let another spirit tie you! Raise your hand, open your mouth and cry out to God, "RELEASE!”

Taking Back Her Soul

After Shelly wrote this letter of admission and released those past hurts, she could at that moment feel herself living that present moment and preparing for her future. She finally had the answer to why she didn't herself. She had come to realize that what she once thought was living was actually a life of dead walking. Shelly began to write more and more about her trials and shared them abroad Face book, Associated Content, Twitter, YouTube and everywhere else she had an account. For anyone who listens she would advise and tell her story to because she wanted other young women to either not go through the situations or get out of the situations. Shelly wanted to be an example of a good ending to all of the untold troubles women face on a daily basis. Shelly wanted to show that no matter what it is that binds you in your spirit and soul; the seal can be broken and you can escape. Shelly stood affirmed and steadfast in producing a life of change. Shelly became a strong woman who released her past, raised her self esteem and stood until God revealed her husband. No longer was she sleeping around and accepting anything and anybody in her life for the purpose of love. Shelly realized that her searching for love went beyond getting raped that it actually starting with not getting a hug from her father or having him tell her he loved her. She realized she had been searching for something she could not find in a man and that was "SELF LOVE, GODLY LOVE!" Shelly lives her life to this day as an advocate for women who want to change bad relationships, habits, mental desecration due from abuse and more. Shelly now lives as a writer who shares the emotions of her trials and stand as a witness of God that all trouble is overcome, taking her soul back and never again holding so much inside.

www.ingramcontent.com/pod-product-compliance
Ingram Content Group UK Ltd.
Pitfield, Milton Keynes, MK11 3LW, UK
UKHW051134260726
13967UKWH00010B/3047

9 781105 117404